Spiritual Gifts

A Bible-based Guide to Understanding and Activating Spiritual Gifts

SPIRITUAL GIFTS

Published by Kindle Direct Publishing
Edited by Anitra Elmore, Jim Laffoon, and David Liauw
Cover design and layout by Eleanor Design Co.

CONTENTS

Foreward

I first met Reggie over two decades ago, when he was a student at the University of North Carolina at Chapel Hill, and I have watched him grow into an incredible Christian, wonderful husband, and great dad. He is also a gifted pastor, leader, and prophetic minister. Over the past decade, Reggie and I have ministered together throughout the United States and around the world, yet it is neither his incredible leadership ability nor the amazing ways God's Spirit operates in him which truly define him. It is Reggie's passion—and God-given ability—to equip the people of God to find and flow in their spiritual gifts. In my opinion, Reggie's life and ministry embody the reality of Ephesians 4:11-12—"So Christ himself gave the apostles, the prophets, the evangelists, the pastors and teachers, to equip his people for works of service, so that the body of Christ may be built up" (Ephesians 4:11-12).

Reggie has lived to equip others, even from his earliest ministry years. I will never forget one of the first times I visited the Every Nation Campus Ministry at Duke University which he and his wife Bomi were leading. Unlike some young leaders who would have sought to impress me with their anointing and stage presence, Reggie did not say a word until the end of the meeting, when he thanked me for coming. What I saw instead was a virtual parade of empowered students who led every aspect of the meeting. God continued to use Reggie in the following years—to equip and empower hundreds of college students to find and flow in their spiritual gifts. We co-founded the Every Nation School of Empowerment to help on a larger scale. I realized, however, Reggie's gift to "equip the saints" had no borders, as I witnessed men and women being empowered around the world.

In this book, you have a practical guide to finding and fulfilling the spiritual gifts God has given you. Although SPIRITUAL GIFTS was originally designed for small group study, it can also be used for one-on-one discipleship as well as personal enrichment. As you read and reread its contents and faithfully practice its recommended exercises, I believe this book may well prove to be the fuse which God will use to ignite His gifts and power in you!

Introduction

We cannot underestimate the sacrificial crucifixion of Jesus Christ for all humanity. Through the cross, Jesus made it possible for us to be in a relationship with the Heavenly Father and to have eternal life. Additionally, His blood and His resurrection makes available the gifts of the Holy Spirit for all believers[1]. And, since Jesus has these gifts for us, we must be willing to receive them, activate them in our lives and not allow them to lay dormant.

Paul gives the Corinthian church and every believer the command to "eagerly desire spiritual gifts," so the body of Christ can be strengthened, encouraged, and comforted.[2] This is also significant for those who don't know God, as it gives them tangible proof, signs, and wonders that point to His existence and love for them. Pointing individuals to Jesus is the mission of the church and it requires the gifts of the Holy Spirit. Paul emphasized this when sharing what God had done through him to the Roman church. He says, "For I will not venture to speak of anything except what Christ has accomplished through me to bring the Gentiles to obedience—by word and deed, by the power of signs and wonders, by the power of the Spirit of God—so that from Jerusalem and all the way around to Illyricum I have fulfilled the

---

1 Ephesians 4 : 7 - 9
2 1 Corinthians 14:1-3

ministry of the gospel of Christ.[3] The author of Hebrews confirms this as well, saying, "[The gospel] was declared at first by the Lord, and it was attested to us by those who heard, while God also bore witness by signs and wonders and various miracles and by the gifts of the Holy Spirit distributed according to his will."[4]

In light of the vital role of gifts in the church's gospel mission, this study is an introduction to the spiritual gifts, which are often referred to as the miraculous gifts or manifestation gifts. We will explore the definition of each gift, see them at work in the Bible, and discover how to activate them according to God's will. And, while this guide is not a comprehensive study on spiritual gifts, it will provide a fundamental understanding of the gifts and how they work. Those of you who've never heard of the gifts of the Holy Spirit will receive an excellent foundation to begin to practice them. Those experienced with the gifts of the Holy Spirit will be encouraged and challenged to grow in them.
A word of caution: Paul tells us to desire spiritual gifts eagerly, yet our primary and greatest desire should be a connection with the gift giver, in the person of God, the Father, Jesus Christ, the Son, and the Holy Spirit.

As you complete this study, keep in mind that when God gives us gifts, he doesn't ask us to work for them. This is as true for spiritual gifts as it is for the gift of salvation and the gift of the Holy Spirit.[5] Salvation is a free gift that Jesus makes available to us when we turn from living for ourselves and acknowledge Him as Lord and Savior ("Lord" means He is the boss of our lives). The spiritual gifts are gifts of grace, which is God's divine favor and

---

3 Romans 15:18-29
4 Hebrews 2:3-4
5 Romans 5:15 & 6:23, Luke 11:13, Acts 2:38

power for us. We don't earn them by being full-time vocational ministers or super Christians. At the same time, they do not indicate how mature a believer is and they don't make one Christ-follower better than another.

Here are a few instructions as you begin. Although you can use this resource for personal enrichment, it is meant primarily for small groups and with the blessing of your church leadership. Groups are better for activations. Gifts are meant for the church and should be under the guidance of church leadership. When reading the Scriptures listed, we recommend that you read through the entire chapter to have a better grasp of the context of whole passages, even though we'll only look at portions of them here. Finally, as you explore the use of these gifts as a group, every person must agree to be truthful yet kind, considerate, courteous, humble, and very patient. Each person should also give room for people to make mistakes. The best environment for this study is one filled with faith in God's ability to help, a desire to honor and please Him, and a love for people. As the apostle, Paul says, "Pursue love, and earnestly desire the spiritual gifts..."[6]

---

6 1 Corinthians 14:1 ESV

Getting Started

"But you will receive power when the Holy Spirit comes on you; and you will be my witnesses in Jerusalem, and in all Judea and Samaria, and to the ends of the earth." Acts 1:8 NIV

You will get the most out of this Bible study and application tool when you are open to God expressing His power through you in various ways. Our openness depends largely on our attitude and our mindset about God and the Bible. In light of this it is important to note that there are different purposes and functions for the variety of gifts mentioned in the Bible and there are different categories of gifts as well. There is also a distinction in the accessibility and availability of gifts. For example, salvation is a spiritual gift that is available to all and it encompasses all the blessings that God offers us through Jesus Christ.[1] Salvation (or eternal life) does not belong in the same category of gifts as celibacy, which is the gift to remain unmarried and accomplish much for the Lord.[2] Salvation is for everyone who believes in Jesus but celibacy is not.

In Paul's writings alone, we find different categories of gifts (see Different Categories of Spiritual Gifts chart in the appendix). In

1 Ephesians 1, 2:6-8 & Romans 6:23
2 1 Corinthians 7:7

Ephesians 4:1-13, he shares a category of giftings that Jesus gives to the Body of Christ. These gifts have the purpose and function of establishing a person's ministry calling and impact in the body of Christ. Paul uses the word klesis[3] (calling) to frame this category of gifts. A believer will not be all of these but will primarily he or she will be one of these.

In Romans 12:4-8, Paul shares a category of spiritual gifts that deal with how a person will practice his or her service. The word he uses to describe these gifts is praxis[4] (action). Christ followers will primarily have one of these gifts.

In 1 Corinthians 12:7-11, Paul introduces another set of gifts that have to do with the power that believers have to fulfill God's mission. This category of gifts is known as the manifestation gifts, and Paul uses the word phanerosis[5] (manifestation) to describe them. For this category of gifts, the Holy Spirit gives us access to all of them. Although we may primarily practice a few of them on a regular basis, the Holy Spirit can choose to allow us to exercise as many of these gifts as He desires. The actual gift is power[6] from the Holy Spirit manifested in many ways who makes all of the gifts in this category available to us as He will. God distributes[7] these gifts many times in combination with each other because that is what is required to produce a particular manifestation that He is seeking.

For example, the gifts of prophecy, words of wisdom, and words of knowledge are often used together to manifest God's comfort and encouragement towards His people.

---

3 Dictionary of Biblical Languages with Semantic Domains: Greek (NT) #3104
4 Dictionary of Biblical Languages with Semantic Domains: Greek (NT) #4552
5 Dictionary of Biblical Languages with Semantic Domains: Greek (NT) #5748
6 Acts 1:8 & Luke 24:49
7 1 Corinthians 12:11

Other manifestations may be healing, deliverance, comfort, strengthening or miracles and more, but they are all for the common good.[8]

Since the focus of this study is the manifestation gifts and not the other ones, we can be open to the Holy Spirit distributing whatever gifts He wants so He can manifest His desire through us. We can trust what Jesus promised His disciples and every Christ-follower: You shall receive power when the Holy Spirit comes to be His witnesses to the world! I encourage you to be receptive and open to the Holy Spirit as you read every chapter and participate in every activation in this book.

8 1 Corinthians 12:7

The Manifestation Gifts

1

> *"To each is given the manifestation of the Spirit for the common good." 1 Corinthians 12:7 ESV*

Warm-up:

What makes a gift special? Share answers within the group, as we begin our study on the special gifts Jesus has given us.

Spotlight:

The manifestation gifts include the following: message or word of wisdom, message or word of knowledge, distinguishing or discerning between spirits, faith, miraculous powers or working of miracles, gifts of healing, prophecy, various kinds of tongues, and interpretation of tongues.

Read:

1 Corinthians 12:4-11 NIV

"There are different kinds of gifts, but the same Spirit distributes them. There are different kinds of service, but the same Lord. There are different kinds of working, but in all of them and in everyone it is the same God at work. Now to each one the manifestation of the Spirit is given for the common good. To one there is given through the Spirit a message of wisdom, to another a message of knowledge by means of the same Spirit, to another faith by the

> same Spirit, to another gifts of healing by that one Spirit, to another miraculous powers, to another prophecy, to another distinguishing between spirits, to another speaking in different kinds of tongues, and to still another the interpretation of tongues. All these are the work of one and the same Spirit, and he distributes them to each one, just as he determines." (Also read 1 Corinthians 12:1-11; 14:1, 4, 24-25, Acts 2:1-4.)

Discover:

The specific focus of this study will be the manifestation gifts that Jesus graciously gives. The word manifestation means "to show or display" and, in this case, it means "to display God's supernatural power." The gifts that Paul mentions in the text are the message of wisdom, the message of knowledge, distinguishing between spirits, faith, miraculous powers, gifts of healing, prophecy, different kinds of tongues, and interpretation of tongues. Although we can identify each of these manifestation gifts individually, in almost every instance, they work together. When the gifts work together, they produce a specific supernatural effect or manifestation that God desires, such as healing, deliverance, salvation, and miracles. We see an example of this when Jesus uses the gifts of faith, miracles, and healings to bring Lazarus back from the dead in John 11:38-44 and again when Jesus uses distinguishing between spirits, healings, and miracles to heal a sick woman in Luke 13:10-13.

The manifestation gifts of the Holy Spirit, who is the third person in the Trinity, have one purpose: to bring people closer to God and His loving intentions for them. This purpose applies to the Christ-follower and those who do not know God, as evidenced below.

1. They can edify or build up individual believers or the entire local congregation.

   "Anyone who speaks in a tongue edifies themselves, but the one who prophesies edifies the church."
   1 Corinthians 14:4 NIV

2. The Holy Spirit can use these gifts to convince those who do not follow Christ of many things. He can use them to convince people to turn from their sin, that Jesus is God, that He was raised from the dead, and continues to reign actively as King of the universe.

   "But if an unbeliever or an inquirer comes in while everyone is prophesying, they are convicted of sin and are brought under judgment by all, as the secrets of their hearts are laid bare. So they will fall down and worship God, exclaiming, 'God is really among you!'" 1 Corinthians 14:24-25 NIV

Paul explains three ways we should approach the manifestation gifts.

1. We should seek to understand what they are and how they work. This study will help you with that.

   "Now about the gifts of the Spirit, brothers, and sisters, I do not want you to be uninformed." 1 Corinthians 12:1 NIV

2. Love must be our motivation as we use these gifts. Many have hurt themselves or others with self-centered motives, such as seeking prestige, money, or self-worth. We run the danger of finding our identity in our gifts

rather than in being sons or daughters of our loving Heavenly Father. Our motivation should be rooted in God's love, His desire to see people whole, and our desire to live a godly life. It's God's love that makes these gifts unique.

"If I speak in the tongues of men or of angels, but do not have love, I am only a resounding gong or a clanging cymbal." 1 Corinthians 13:1 NIV

3. Paul urges us to long for and seek to become active in the spiritual gifts, especially prophecy. This urging from Paul means we can confidently ask our Heavenly Father for any of these manifestation gifts. When we ask Him, He will distribute them based on what He wants to do through us in a specific situation for His glory!

   "Follow the way of love and eagerly desire gifts of the Spirit, especially prophecy." 1 Corinthians 14:1 NIV

Application

Reflect:

1. What resonated most with you from this Bible study?

2. Have you received the free gift of salvation? If you would like to receive the gift of salvation purchased by Jesus' life, death, and resurrection, please find the appendix in the back and pray the salvation prayer.

3. If you haven't received the Baptism in the Holy Spirit, the next chapter will focus on that topic and you'll have an opportunity to receive God's power through spiritual gifts.

Pray:
You will need humility and courage to begin or continue to practice the spiritual gifts.
In your own words, pray that God will help you to humble yourself and be open to receive spiritual gifts without being afraid to make a mistake and without comparing yourself to others. Now, ask God to give you the courage by His Holy Spirit to become active in using these gifts to bring people closer to Jesus.

Baptism of The Holy Spirit

2

"John answered them all, 'I baptize you with water...He will baptize you with the Holy Spirit and fire.'" Luke 3:16 NIV

Warm-up:

What are some benefits of electrical or gas power? Share answers within the group, as we consider the benefits of spiritual power.

Spotlight:

When we put our faith in Christ, God dwells in us and yet He grants us a distinct and ongoing experience with the Holy Spirit. God does this through the baptism of the Holy Spirit, who as the third person of the Trinity provides physical manifestations of power to increase our ability to share and show the good news of Jesus Christ.

Read:

Acts 1:5,8 NIV
"For John baptized with water, but in a few days you will be baptized with the Holy Spirit."

"But you will receive power when the Holy Spirit comes on you, and you will be my witnesses in Jerusalem, and in all Judea and Samaria, and to the ends of the earth."

Acts 19:1-2, 6 NIV
"...There he found some disciples and asked them, 'Did you receive the Holy Spirit when you believed?' They answered, 'No, we have not even heard that there is a Holy Spirit.'"
"When Paul placed his hands on them, the Holy Spirit came on them, and they spoke in tongues and prophesied."

Discover:
Everything in Jesus' story shows us that God desires to reveal Himself to others through His power. Jesus was born through a supernatural virgin birth, and lived a perfect life, free from sin. Jesus healed the sick, delivered the oppressed, and raised the dead. He died on the cross to restore humanity to God the Father, and God miraculously raised Him from the dead[1]. After His resurrection, Jesus appeared to His disciples and breathed the Holy Spirit into their hearts, drawing a parallel to the way God formed Adam with his breath in the creation story[2]. The breath of the Holy Spirit regenerated them with eternal life and connected them back to God. God opened the eyes of the disciples to the gospel, and they then became genuine followers of Christ[3].

Although the Holy Spirit regenerated the disciples, they were missing the power that God desired to give them as a gift. This gift of power would allow them to tangibly show the world that God was real and that Jesus was the risen and reigning Lord. Not long after the Holy Spirit started to live in the hearts of the disciples, Jesus commanded His followers to stay in Jerusalem before going out to share

---

1 Matthew 1:18-25; 2 Corinthians 5:21; Ephesians 2:1-10; Romans 1:2-4
2 Genesis 2:7 ; John 20:19-23
3 John 3:1-8, 20:9; Luke 24:36-45

the gospel[4]. He told them instead to wait until they had another experience with the Holy Spirit. This subsequent experience is called the outpouring of the Spirit, filling of the Spirit or baptism of the Holy Spirit[5]. After that command, Jesus ascended to His throne in heaven, and for roughly ten days, these genuine Christ-followers waited for this promise by praying and praising God[6]. While they gathered for the Jewish celebration called Pentecost, Jesus poured out His Spirit from heaven, and His followers received the baptism of the Holy Spirit.

This baptism of the Holy Spirit, which is still available today, gives followers of Christ the ability to supernaturally display the gospel of the kingdom through bold speech and spiritual gifts[7]. It's a recurring theme in the book of Acts, where the primary evidence of the baptism of the Holy Spirit is people speaking in an unlearned tongue or heavenly language and prophesying words prompted by God[8]. In Acts 19:1-7, disciples in Ephesus had not heard that there was a baptism or outpouring of the Holy Spirit. So, Paul shares the good news more fully with them. He water-baptized them in the name of Jesus, and laid his hands on them to receive the baptism of the Holy Spirit. They received the power to be witnesses to the world for the glory of Jesus Christ. Like electrical or gas power, this power brings light and is beneficial to many.

4 Luke 24:36-49
5 Acts 1:4-8
6 Acts 1:6-14 & Luke 24:49-53
7 Acts 2:1-11
8 Acts 2:1-4, Acts 8:14-24, Acts 9:17-18 10:44-48, Acts 19:1-7

Application

Reflect:

1. Have you been baptized in the Holy Spirit?

2. Have you ever had visible supernatural displays of God's power when you serve, pray for, or share God's word with others?

3. Have you ever verbally communicated in an unlearned language directly to God from your spirit through your mouth without the aid of your mind?

Pray:
If you would like to receive the baptism of the Holy Spirit, have people in your small group lay hands on you and ask God to baptize you in His Spirit.

Pray this prayer below:
Heavenly Father, I believe you are a good God who gives good gifts (Luke 11:13)! I am asking You for the gift of Your Holy Spirit. According to Your promise, please baptize me in the Holy Spirit and release your supernatural power in my life.

Activate:
Now you are going to allow the Holy Spirit to prompt you to speak in a language or words that you have not learned.

Relax (you may consider taking a deep breath). Immediately after you relax, start to express out loud what you feel or sense the Holy Spirit is prompting you to say. Your words should be in a language that is not aided by your mind but is unlearned. Please submit to the Holy Spirit by taking a step of faith to speak out of your mouth as the disciples did in Acts 2:4, when they uttered what they felt the Spirit gave them. Someone should end with a prayer and blessing over the group.

The Gifts & God's Voice

3

"Now concerning spiritual gifts, brothers, I do not want you to be uninformed. You know that when you were pagans you were led astray to mute idols, however, you were led."
1 Corinthians 12:1-2 ESV

Warm-up:
Why is communication critical to accomplishing a task between coworkers? Share answers within the group, as we discuss the importance of hearing God's voice.

Spotlight:
God's communication to us can release the gifts of the Holy Spirit through us.

Read:

Acts 8:29-30 ESV
"And the Spirit said to Philip, 'Go over and join this chariot.' So Philip ran to him and heard him reading Isaiah the prophet and asked, 'Do you understand what you are reading?'"

Acts 9:10-11 ESV
"Now there was a disciple at Damascus named Ananias. The Lord said to him in a vision, 'Ananias.' And he said, 'Here

I am, Lord.' And the Lord said to him, 'Rise and go to the street called Straight, and at the house of Judas look for a man of Tarsus named Saul, for behold, he is praying'"

Acts 15:28 ESV
"For it has seemed good to the Holy Spirit and to us to lay on you no greater burden than these requirements..."

Discover:
When Paul writes about the manifestation gifts in 1 Corinthians 12, he begins by making it clear how spiritual gifts work. He contrasts how they lived before they were Christ-followers, when they worshipped false gods or idols that were not real and could not communicate. He explains that as Christ-followers, they were to no longer be without understanding as they were before. Instead, he instructed the Corinthian believers to recognize that the gifts work as the only true God moves upon them and communicates in various ways. We can call God's communication to us personal revelation. It is so important that we learn to recognize God's communication since His revelation releases the gifts of the Spirit.

We see examples of this in the passages we read above from the book of Acts. God gave personal revelation and released faith and boldness to Phillip to share the Good news of Jesus Christ to the high ranking Ethiopian Eunuch. Philip received this personal revelation as the Holy Spirit moved upon his mind, communicating through thoughts and phrases to him.

God gave Ananias personal revelation through a vision. Visions typically occur by personal revelation when God moves on the screen of your imagination, and He shows you a picture or something like a video clip of what He wants to communicate. In this case, God gave Ananias a personal revelation about the location and activities of a man he was to meet. This vision led him to Saul (another name for Paul) and he went on to play a pivotal part in Paul's story. (We'll explore that in another chapter.)

Then there are the apostles and elders in the Jerusalem council in Acts 15. Through the communication of the Holy Spirit, they were able to exercise the gift of wisdom through personal revelation. The Holy Spirit gave them a revelation regarding how non-Jewish converts could best serve Christ and live in unity with their Jewish brothers and sisters. They received this revelation, not only through hearing the communications of the Holy Spirit, but also feeling His pleasure. As the Holy Spirit moved on their emotions, and they felt or sensed that He endorsed their decision, they were able to say that "it seemed good to the Holy Spirit and us." God is alive and gives personal revelation in a number of ways. He releases His gifts through us by moving upon our minds to communicate a thought or phrase. He also communicates through visions as he moves upon the screens of our imagination. Or perhaps He moves on our emotions, as we feel His approval or disapproval about a situation.

Application

Reflect:

1. Based on the reading, what is the vital connection between receiving personal revelation through God's communication and spiritual gifts?

2. Out of the three modes of personal revelation listed, which one is the primary way you seem to receive God's communications?

3. Would you like to share any personal stories related to hearing God's voice?

Pray:

Heavenly Father, I am grateful that You are real, You are alive, and You communicate. Please speak to me now and let me know Your heart, desires, and will.

Activate:

Let's take a moment to listen to the communications of God. Either pray softly in the Spirit or be silent. As you are quiet or praying in tongues, look for God to communicate by moving on your mind with a thought (perhaps a scripture may come to your mind). Also, look for God to move on the screen of your imagination and show you a vision. Your eyes can be opened or closed, depending on how you best focus. Or, maybe look for God to move on your emotions as you feel and sense His heart in a particular situation. As you listen to the communications of God please know that they will not contradict the character of God or biblical scriptures. After listening to God's communications, take a moment, if you feel comfortable, and share what you received.

Different Kinds of Tongues

4

"...to another speaking in different kinds of tongues..."
1 Corinthians 12:10 NIV

Warm-up:

How do you decide what to pray? Share answers within the group as we uncover a powerful way to pray for others.

Spotlight:

Through the gift of tongues, God grants us the ability to speak words that bypass natural reason and logic. These words can be either a prayer, message from God in a known human language, or an unintelligible heavenly language. God will use this gift to strengthen a Christ-follower's faith, help them to pray powerfully for others, or as a message to be interpreted for fellow Christ-followers.

Read:

Acts 2:1-4 NIV

"When the day of Pentecost came, they were all together in one place. Suddenly a sound like the blowing of a violent wind came from heaven and filled the whole house where they were sitting. They saw what seemed to be tongues of fire that separated and came to rest on each of them. All of them were filled with the Holy Spirit and began to speak in

other tongues as the Spirit enabled them."

1 Corinthians 14:2 NIV
"For anyone who speaks in a tongue does not speak to people but to God. Indeed, no one understands them; they utter mysteries by the Spirit."

1 Corinthians 14:4-5 NIV
"Anyone who speaks in a tongue edifies themselves, but the one who prophesies edifies the church. I would like every one of you to speak in tongues, but I would rather have you prophesy. The one who prophesies is greater than the one who speaks in tongues, unless someone interprets, so that the church may be edified."

1 Corinthians 14:13-15 NIV
For this reason, the one who speaks in a tongue should pray that they may interpret what they say. For if I pray in a tongue, my spirit prays, but my mind is unfruitful. So what shall I do? I will pray with my spirit, but I will also pray with my understanding; I will sing with my spirit, but I will also sing with my understanding."

Discover:
In this passage in Acts 2, it had been roughly ten days since the disciples had seen Jesus ascend into heaven before their very eyes. Jesus told them to wait to receive a special endowment of power from Him before they went out to share the gospel with the world. In those ten days, they were continuously praying, waiting expectantly for something to happen. The tenth day marked the Jewish celebration of Pentecost or the ingathering feast of weeks for harvest. On that day, the Holy Spirit was poured out on them as prophesied about Jesus and brought understanding

to a passage in the book of Joel[1].

Here we see that the very first gift God bestowed upon the 120 disciples gathered in prayer was the gift of speaking in tongues. They felt and sensed the heat and wind of the Holy Spirit moving upon them and in their souls. They cooperated with the Holy Spirit by taking a step of faith to vocalize words that they had never learned before. On that day, those who heard the sound of the wind gathered to see what was happening, and they heard the disciples speaking in human languages. Speaking in human languages is one aspect of the gift called speaking in different kinds of tongues. God strengthened the disciples to share the gospel boldly, fully inspired by the Holy Spirit with untaught words.

Years later, the apostle Paul would offer the Corinthian church more insights on the various expressions of tongues. In 1 Corinthians 14, he affirms the manifestation of tongues that the disciples experienced on Pentecost[2]. He then goes on to share another aspect of the gift of tongues which involves words of prayer that are directed to God and not meant for humans to understand. This demonstration of the gift is called praying in the spirit. This prayer language of never before learned words has the extraordinary ability to edify or build up personal faith and to help us intercede powerfully on behalf of others[3]. This aspect of the gift of tongues gives us a connection with God that allows us to pray impactfully even when we don't know how to pray.

---

1 Acts 1:4-5, 2:15-21 & Joel 2:28-32
2 1 Corinthians 14:20-22
3 Jude 20-21 Romans 8:26-28

Paul shares that another kind of expression concerning this gift is to give praise to God by singing in these untaught words. Lastly, he explains how tongues can be used as a message from God to a church gathering when God initiates the gift of tongues combined with the gift of interpretation. This demonstration of the gift strengthens, encourages, and comforts the body of believers, just like prophecy.

It's clear from these passages that the various expressions of tongues are extremely beneficial when we understand how to use them. The different kinds of tongues are beautiful gifts that propel us more into God's glory and purpose, and this is why Paul encourages us to use them, saying, "Therefore, my brothers and sisters, be eager to prophesy, and do not forbid speaking in tongues."[4]

Application

Reflect:

1. What does the gift of various kinds of tongues reveal about God?

2. In what ways could this gift be beneficial for you and those around you?

4 1 Corinthians 14:39 NIV

3. Would you like to share any personal stories related to this gift?

Pray:
Heavenly Father, through the power of the Holy Spirit, please activate the gift of various kinds of tongues in my life (or make it stronger in my life). Please use this gift for Your glory and the benefit of others, just like You did in the churches in Acts and just as Paul instructed. In Jesus' name, I pray, amen.

Activate:
Each person should choose one of the following to focus on while praying in tongues/praying in the spirit: A challenging situation, a family member, or a friend.

Everyone should then take 5-10 minutes to pray in the spirit simultaneously. Someone can start, and someone can end the prayer time by praying a blessing over the moment of prayer. Afterward, each person can share what he or she felt, saw, heard, or sensed from God during their time of prayer. We encourage each person to practice this exercise at home as much as possible.

to see him. "Then he said [prophesied]: 'The God of our ancestors has chosen you to know his will and to see the Righteous One and to hear words from his mouth. You will be his witness to all people of what you have seen and heard." (parentheses added. Also see Acts 9:10-17)

1 Timothy 4:14 NIV
"Do not neglect your gift, which was given you through prophecy when the body of elders laid their hands on you."

1 Corinthians 14:24-25 NIV
"But if an unbeliever or an inquirer comes in while everyone is prophesying, they are convicted of sin and are brought under judgment by all, as the secrets of their hearts are laid bare. So they will fall down and worship God, exclaiming, "God is really among you!"

Discover:
When God uses an individual to communicate His heart for people and His plan for them, this is called prophecy. In 1 Corinthians, Paul explains that the purpose of the gift of prophecy is threefold: This gift builds God's people up to display God's glory, it gives them the courage to live out God's plan, and it brings warning and comfort as they face challenges and suffering.

The apostle Paul was very familiar with this gift. When he first declared his faith in Christ, and began his ministry, he received prophetic encouragement, strengthening, and comfort from a disciple named Ananias. Although there was no indication that Ananias was in full-time vocational ministry, he exercised the gift of prophecy, which was activated as he prayed. As the Holy Spirit moved on Ananias' mind, he experienced a vision and heard a prophetic message. He shared that message with Paul, telling him that God had chosen him to know His will, to see the Righteous One, and to hear words from His mouth. He also prophesied that Paul's life would provide proof to many people that Christ Jesus is risen and reigning. Paul's personal experience with prophecy affirmed God's love for him and confirmed God's call on his life. This prophetic word also foretold his future, bringing assurance, as prophecies often do.

The gift of prophecy was continually evident throughout Paul's ministry. His first ministry partner was Barnabas — he had a strong gift of prophecy and his name means "son of prophecy or encouragement[1]."

During Paul's ministry, he traveled to Jerusalem to deliver relief during a famine. Paul encountered the gift of prophecy in every city he visited along his journey[2] and the famine had been predicted by the prophet, Agabus, in Acts 11:27-30. The Holy Spirit told Paul prophetically that he would experience challenges when he went to Jerusalem. Through the gift of prophecy members of the church in every city Paul started a congregation confirmed the message that challenges awaited Paul in Jerusalem.

While Paul is in Caesarea, the prophet, Agabus, encouraged the church, giving Paul the same prophetic word he'd heard in the cities he had traveled to and adding more details.[3]

---

1 Strong's Concise Dictionary of Greek Testament & the Hebrew Bible -Barnabas is Greek word # 921 derived from Hebrew words bar # 1247 means son & naba #5012 to prophesy

2 Acts 20:22 - 23

3 Acts 21:10 -15

These prophecies foretold the bonds and afflictions that awaited Paul and what was revealed through the gift of prophecy was fulfilled in his life in Acts 21:27-33.

Paul also witnessed the gift of prophecy at work when the elders laid hands on Timothy, his spiritual son. The Holy Spirit gave these elders messages of upbuilding and encouragement that revealed God's heart and activated God's gift in young Timothy. This gift allowed Timothy to be effective in sharing and showing the gospel to people. One more profound way that Paul witnessed the gift of prophecy was in evangelism with those who did not know God[4]. In this expression of the gift, secrets of individuals' hearts and lives were revealed as a sign and wonder, pointing to the reality that Jesus Christ is real and alive!

Application

Reflect:

1. What does the gift of the prophecy reveal about God?

2. In what ways could this gift be beneficial for you and those around you?

---

4 1Corinthians 14:25

3. Would you like to share any personal stories related to this gift?

Pray:
Heavenly Father, please activate the gift of prophecy in my life (or make it stronger in my life) by the power of the Holy Spirit. Let this gift glorify You and build up, strengthen, and comfort Your sons and daughters. Please use this gift to reach those who don't know you. In Jesus' name, I pray, amen.

Activate:
Find a partner, preferably one you do not know very well. During this exercise, you will both ask God to reveal a specific and relevant prophetic message for your partner. Here are a few things to remember as you activate this gift:

- This activation is practice, so it's okay if you make a mistake.
- Please remember to speak encouraging, strengthening, and comforting words only (avoid demeaning or manipulative words).
- To provide a safe environment for prophecy, we encourage you not to share certain words. We discourage predictive words on who and when to marry, pregnancies or the future number of children, and directives about changing careers. Also, it is crucial to note that prophecy will not contradict the character of God or biblical scriptures.
- Lastly, you should share any prophetic words you receive

with pastors, spiritual leaders, and those who are spiritually mature. These individuals will be able to test them and help you apply them correctly in your life.

Begin to pray in the spirit and ask the Holy Spirit to reveal God's heart for the person, related to his or her past, present, or future. Wait a few minutes for Him to speak to you.

Now each person should take a few minutes to share what they hear, see, or feel. When we ask God to be involved, He moves on our souls, and prophetic words are usually the first things that we sense or come to mind. End by praying a blessing over the person, even if you didn't feel you received a prophetic word. Someone should end the time with a prayer and blessing over the group.

Interpretation of Tongues

6

"...to still another the interpretation of tongues."
1 Corinthians 12:10 NIV

Warm-up:
Why is it helpful to understand what people communicate to us? Share answers within the group as we discover the importance of interpretation of tongues.

Spotlight:
Through the gift of interpretation of tongues, God grants a Christ-follower the ability to understand a message spoken through the gift of tongues and to explain that message to others.

Read:

1 Corinthians 14:5 NIV
"I would like every one of you to speak in tongues, but I would rather have you prophesy. The one who prophesies is greater than the one who speaks in tongues, unless someone interprets, so that the church may be edified."

1 Corinthians 14:12-13 NIV
"So it is with you. Since you are eager for gifts of the Spirit, try to excel in those that build up the church. For this

reason, the one who speaks in a tongue should pray that they may interpret what they say."

1 Corinthians 14:26-28 NIV
"What then shall we say, brothers and sisters? When you come together, each of you has a hymn, or a word of instruction, a revelation, a tongue or an interpretation. Everything must be done so that the church may be built up. If anyone speaks in a tongue, two—or at the most three—should speak, one at a time and someone must interpret. If there is no interpreter, the speaker should keep quiet in the church and speak to himself and to God."

Discover:
Paul was the lead church planter of a spirit-filled congregation in Corinth that operated regularly in the manifestation gifts of the Holy Spirit. Although the members of the congregation were gifted, they were not orderly. In their disorder, they created hindrances that impeded spiritual progress for those who didn't know God or were not familiar with the gifts of the Holy Spirit. Paul's letter to the Corinthians offers instruction on how to keep order in local church gatherings like those that typically happen on Sundays, although the average church gathering was in the home. These public gatherings, which have both believers and nonbelievers in attendance are meant for worship and biblical teaching. It's important to note that Paul was not writing about prayer gatherings, gatherings where believers are being equipped, or private devotional moments. When you understand that, it is easy to see why he emphasized prophecy over speaking in tongues, as tongues are less intelligible and do not give the hearers an understanding of the gospel and God's love.

Paul goes on to explain that when the gift of tongues is accompanied by interpretation, it becomes intelligible and has the same effect as prophecy—offering encouragement, strengthening, and comfort for Christ-followers. Paul says the gift of interpretation should be combined with the particular aspect of the gift of tongues where it is a message from God to the church. Paul saw this gift in operation as a few people spoke in tongues, and as others listened to God's communication. Those who operated in the gift of interpretation would discern what the Holy Spirit was saying through phrases in their minds, visions on the screen of their imaginations, impressions in their feelings, and other ways. They would then share what God communicated to build up the church. Paul encourages anyone who speaks in tongues in the forefront of the church gathering to also pray that they will interpret the tongues so they can give an understandable message to everyone. The gift of interpretation allows all who are present to understand God's truth and love.

Application

Reflect:

1. What does the gift of the interpretation of tongues reveal about God?

2. In what ways could this gift be beneficial for you and those around you?

3. Would you like to share any personal stories related to this gift?

Pray:
Heavenly Father, through the power of the Holy Spirit, please activate the gift of interpretation of tongues in my life (or make it stronger in my life). Please let me use it in an orderly way, for Your glory and the benefit of people just like You did throughout the churches in Acts, especially in Corinth. In Jesus' name, I pray, amen.

Activate:
As we seek to activate the gift of the interpretation of tongues, let's remember some of the guidelines for prophecy since these gifts have the same goal of building up the church through strengthening, encouragement, and comfort.

- This activation is practice, so it's okay if you make a mistake.
- Please remember to speak encouraging, strengthening, and comforting words only (avoid demeaning or

manipulative words).

- We discourage predictive words on who and when to marry, pregnancies or the future number of children, and directives about changing careers. Also, it is crucial to note that prophecy will not contradict the character of God or biblical scriptures.
- What we interpret should be submitted to pastors and those who are spiritually mature for judgment and proper application.

First, have as many people as possible in the group pray in tongues for a few minutes. Whoever feels they have a message in tongues for the group should signal it in some way (raise your hand, stand up, etc.). One person after another should share the message in tongues (we encourage no more than three people to share). At the same time, others are quietly listening to what God is saying. After someone speaks in tongues, one to three others can share what they sense God is revealing as the interpretation. The person speaking in tongues can also ask God for the interpretation. Look for common themes as people share. You are not necessarily looking for a translation but to capture the essence of God's message. End with a prayer and blessing over the group.

Word of Wisdom

7

"To one there is given through the Spirit a message of wisdom..." 1 Corinthians 12:8 NIV

Warm-up:
In what ways are we positively impacted by the wisdom of others? Share answers within the group as we discover the purpose of this gift.

Spotlight:
Through the gift of the message or word of wisdom, God grants us a portion of His supernatural wisdom through the Holy Spirit. God gives this wisdom apart from natural reasoning or reliance on the five senses in order to provide direction and solutions for present and future challenges.

Read:

Acts 6:1-4 NIV

"In those days when the number of disciples was increasing, the Hellenistic Jews among them complained against the Hebraic Jews because their widows were being overlooked in the daily distribution of food. So the Twelve gathered all the disciples together and said, "It would not be right for us to neglect the ministry of the word of God in order to wait on tables. Brothers and sisters, choose seven men

from among you who are known to be full of the Spirit and wisdom. We will turn this responsibility over to them and will give our attention to prayer and the ministry of the word."

Discover:
In this passage in Acts, the number of Christ-followers was increasing throughout Jerusalem and the surrounding areas. This increase in disciples was a direct result of the apostles preaching the gospel, healing the sick, and delivering the demonically oppressed. As they preached the gospel, the power they displayed through signs and wonders caused them to face imprisonment and death threats from governing authorities. Yet, they continued in ministry exercising the gifts of the Holy Spirit and the church continued to grow.

As God added to the church, they experienced an unforeseen issue. The enemy tried to bring division as one group of widows within the church felt the leaders had overlooked them in the food distribution. If the apostles failed to address the matter, it would have hindered growth and injured the church. As the church leaders considered this issue, they received a solution from God through the gift of the word of wisdom. The wisdom given by the Holy Spirit was to appoint spirit-filled leaders in service to handle the distribution. This word of wisdom contained insight and foresight that not only rescued the church from a disaster but also accelerated gospel ministry and led to more significant growth.

This God-inspired solution is similar to the word of wisdom that God gave James in the Jerusalem council to preserve the essence of the gospel and the unity of Jews and non-Jewish Christ-followers.[1] God also gave Elisha a word of wisdom to bring healing to an entire city in crisis.[2] Elisha also received a word of wisdom to help a poor lady avoid being enslaved by creditors.[3] In all these cases and more, this gift reveals the superiority of God's wisdom over man's as well as His loving compassion towards people.

Application

Reflect:

1. What does the gift of the word of wisdom reveal about God?

2. How could you envision this gift working in your home and job?

3. Would you like to share any personal stories related to this gift?

---

1 Acts 15
2 2 Kings 2:19-22
3 2 Kings 3-4

Pray:
Heavenly Father, please activate the gift of the word of wisdom in my life (or make it stronger) by the power of the Holy Spirit. Please let me use this gift for Your glory, and the benefit of others like you did with the early Christ-followers mentioned in Acts.

Activate:
Find a partner and share a problem you or someone else is facing. Take a minute to pray in the spirit as you pray for each other. Ask God for a word of wisdom, a God-inspired solution to a problem the person is facing. Take a minute to share what you believe you have received from God. Whatever solutions you give should not contradict the Bible or God's character. Share the solution you received from your partner with a spiritual leader in your church community for confirmation and further wisdom.

Word of Knowledge

8

"...to another a message of knowledge by means of the same Spirit,"   1 Corinthians 12:8 NIV

Warm-up:
What are some benefits and dangers of possessing knowledge? Share answers within the group as we discover the purpose of this gift.

Spotlight:
Through the gift of the word of knowledge, God supernaturally grants us specific information about people, places, and things (both past and present) that we do not acquire through natural means. It often comes through a vision or God's voice.

Read:

Acts 9:10-12 NIV
"In Damascus, there was a disciple named Ananias. The Lord called to him in a vision, "Ananias!" "Yes, Lord," he answered. The Lord told him, "Go to the house of Judas on Straight Street and ask for a man from Tarsus named Saul, for he is praying. In a vision, he has seen a man named Ananias come and place his hands on him to restore his sight."

Discover:
In Acts, chapter 9, Saul (who was also called Paul) was on his way to Damascus with letters from the high priest in Israel giving him permission to harm Jews that became Christ-followers. Jesus interrupted Paul's trip with a blinding light to reveal to Paul that he was on the wrong side of the battle as a persecutor of God's people.[1] Paul lost his sight during this encounter and his companions helped him continue his journey to Damascus where he remained blind for three days.[2]

During this time, God redirected the prayer time of a man named Ananias, a normal Christ-follower, and spoke to him about Paul. The Lord gave Ananias information that he did not receive through study, the newspaper, or conversation with any other human being or source. God told him he would find Paul praying at Judas' house on the street called Straight. God then explains that Paul had seen a vision of a man laying hands on him to restore his sight. Through the word of knowledge, God tells Ananias what happened to Paul (he'd lost his sight), where he was located and what he was doing at that time. God reveals this to Ananias without him being physically present to see any of this and without any human being telling him.

God shares this information with Ananias even though he was fearful and hesitant about Paul, who had a reputation for hurting Christians. Ananias was not a pastor, preacher, or a prophet. He was an ordinary Christ-following disciple. When he obeyed God and acted on the supernatural

1 Acts 26:9-14
2 Acts 9:8-9

information he received, he showed that God is real and all-knowing. He brought comfort, encouragement, and sobriety to Paul. All of these benefits came as a result of receiving the word of knowledge and acting on it. This also shows us that the word of knowledge is a powerful gift in bringing people to Christ. Ananias' word of knowledge impacted the life and ministry of the Apostle Paul, who would go on to establish dozens of churches and write two-thirds of the New Testament of which we continue to enjoy today.

Application

Reflect:

1. What does the gift of the word of knowledge reveal about God?

2. In what ways could this gift be beneficial for you and those around you?

3. Would you like to share any personal stories related to this gift?

Pray:

Heavenly Father, please activate the gift of the word of knowledge in my life (or make it stronger in my life) by the power of the Holy Spirit. Please let this gift be for Your glory and the benefit of people just like it was for Paul through Ananias. In Jesus' name, I pray, amen.

Activate:

Please take a moment to pair up in your group. Everyone should take a few minutes to pray in the spirit and listen to what God communicates. As you are listening, ask the Holy Spirit to reveal some specific information about the person's past or present that you don't already know to strengthen, encourage, or comfort them. If you received a word of knowledge related to sin or sin patterns please do not share that with the person but share it with their pastor. After you've prayed, then share what you feel is a word of knowledge. Once you've shared the word you believe you received, ask the person if it resonates with them. Conclude your time by praying blessings over them.

Distinguishing of Spirits

9

"...to another distinguishing between spirits."
1 Corinthians 12:10 NIV

Warm-up:
What are the benefits of any filter, whether noise, water, or air? Share answers within the group as we discover the purpose of this gift.

Spotlight:
Through the gift of distinguishing, discerning, or differentiating spirits, God grants us the supernatural ability to perceive whether the source of activities, conditions, and teachings are godly, demonic, or human.

Read:

Acts 16:6-10 NIV

"Paul and his companions traveled throughout the region of Phrygia and Galatia, having been kept by the Holy Spirit from preaching the word in the province of Asia. When they came to the border of Mysia, they tried to enter Bithynia, but the Spirit of Jesus would not allow them to. So they passed by Mysia and went down to Troas. During the night, Paul had a vision of a man of Macedonia standing and begging him, "Come over to Macedonia and help us." After

Paul had seen the vision, we got ready at once to leave for Macedonia, concluding that God had called us to preach the gospel to them.

Acts 16:16-18 NIV

Once when we were going to the place of prayer, we were met by a female slave who had a spirit by which she predicted the future. She earned a great deal of money for her owners by fortune-telling. She followed Paul and the rest of us, shouting, "These men are servants of the Most-High God, who are telling you the way to be saved." She kept this up for many days. Finally, Paul became so annoyed that he turned around and said to the spirit, "In the name of Jesus Christ, I command you to come out of her!" At that moment, the spirit left her.

Discover:

Paul finds himself passing through the province of Asia on a second missionary journey with his team. Although he sincerely desires to share the good news in Asia, he distinguishes that the Holy Spirit does not want him to minister there, yet. Paul and his friends try to enter another city, but the Spirit of Jesus or the Holy Spirit would not let them. God grants Paul the ability to discern that this is not a diabolical delay from Satan but a divine delay from the Holy Spirit. Paul can filter through the noise of life and hear God's direction through the gift of differentiating spirits.

During the night, Paul has a vision of a man calling for him to come to Macedonia. God grants Paul the gift of discerning of spirits to perceive that the source of the vision is the Holy Spirit, and it is God who wants him to move on to Macedonia. Macedonia is where Paul and his companions launch the Philippian church through the power of God and their ministry efforts (Acts 16). This ability to distinguish between spirits gives Paul and his friends insight into God's purpose and plan and protects them from being in the wrong place at the wrong time.

When Paul and his friends arrive in the province of Macedonia in the city of Philippi, he encounters a slave girl who predicts the future. Paul is not a stranger to future predictions since he was very well-read in Old Testament prophecies. When Paul hears her continuously speaking a truthful statement about him and his friends, God grants him the ability to see beyond her words and outward appearance. God uncovers the unseen spiritual forces for Paul, who discerns that this young lady is under the influence of an evil spirit of divination. As a result, he is able to free her, by the power of the Holy Spirit, from this oppressive spirit. Paul's use of the gift of differentiating spirits led to this young lady's freedom, much like Jesus' use of the gift freed a young lady from a spirit of infirmity.[1] God provides freedom, direction, and protection for followers of Christ through the gift of the distinguishing of spirits.

Application

Reflect:

1. What does the gift of the distinguishing of spirits reveal about God?

1 Luke 13:10-13

2. In what ways could this gift be beneficial for you and those around you?

3. Would you like to share any personal stories related to this gift?

Pray:
Heavenly Father, through the power of the Holy Spirit, please activate the gift of the distinguishing of spirits in my life (or make it stronger in my life). Please let this gift be for Your glory and the benefit of people, just like You did for Jesus and Paul, who brought freedom and healing to the soul and body of people. In Jesus' name, I pray, amen.

Activate:
Choose one person in your group. This person will now share the name only of a family member or friend who he or she knows is personally experiencing a spiritual challenge. All others in the group will ask God to help them distinguish if there is a spiritual influence connected to this person's issue. Take a brief moment to pray in the spirit and wait on God's insight. After praying, everyone will take a moment to share what they sensed God was revealing. The person who shared the spiritual challenge will confirm or disconfirm the thoughts shared by the group members. Look for the

common themes that people feel God emphasizes. Now, take a moment to pray for victory and blessing over that person's friend, family member, or their issue. Repeat this with the group at least one more time.

The Gift of Faith

10

"...to another faith by the same Spirit..."
1 Corinthians 12:9 NIV

Warm-up:
What makes us confident about some things and not confident about other things? Share answers within the group as we discover the purpose of this gift.

Spotlight:
Through the gift of faith, God grants us unwavering clarity and confidence that propels us to speak words or to act. These actions release supernatural power to fulfill His will for specific situations.

Read:
Mark 11:22-24 NIV
"Have faith in God," Jesus answered. "Truly I tell you, if anyone says to this mountain, 'Go, throw yourself into the sea,' and does not doubt in their heart but believes that what they say will happen, it will be done for them. Therefore I tell you, whatever you ask for in prayer, believe that you have received it, and it will be yours."(See Mark

chapter 11)

Acts 4:29-31 NIV
"Now, Lord, consider their threats and enable your servants to speak your word with great boldness. Stretch out your hand to heal and perform signs and wonders through the name of your holy servant Jesus." After they prayed, the place where they were meeting was shaken. And they were all filled with the Holy Spirit and spoke the word of God boldly."

Discover:
Jesus was on the road to Jerusalem, where He would face crucifixion. Just days before He would die, He had an important lesson to teach His disciples. He arrived in Jerusalem and passed by a fig tree. He was hungry, but found the tree had no fruit for Him to eat. While standing in front of the fruitless tree, He received the will of the Holy Spirit through a definite impression or word regarding this tree. With unwavering clarity and boldness, He spoke directly to the tree out loud and in front of His disciples, that no one should eat from that tree ever again. His disciples heard this and didn't think much of it. The next morning they all passed by the tree, and saw that it was almost dead and drying up from its roots. The disciples were in awe of what they saw and told Jesus, "Look, what you said is happening." Jesus gave them a lesson in the gift of faith. If you have a type of faith in God that is with complete certainty and without any doubts, which only God can impart to you, then when you speak in His will, what you say will happen. This gift of faith brings you to a place in your soul and spirit in which you totally trust

and believe God. This kind of faith occurs before there is physical confirmation; you believe that you have already received what you asked God for in prayer or when you obeyed Him.

Peter had the same gift of faith imparted to him to walk on water.[1] God infused Peter with clarity on His specific will in that situation and confidence in His power, which produced bold action that resulted in a miracle. The disciples also experienced this gift of faith. It happened when they prayed and the Holy Spirit dispensed the gift of faith to them to boldly preach the gospel in the face of threats and imprisonment in Acts 4. The gift of faith allowed Jesus and His disciples to speak boldly, do the impossible, and release God's will on earth as it is in heaven.

Application

Reflect:

1. What does the gift of faith reveal about God?

2. In what ways could this gift be beneficial for you and those around you?

1 Matthew 14:22-33

3. Would you like to share any personal stories related to this gift?

Pray:

Heavenly Father, please activate the gift of faith in my life (or make it stronger in my life) by the power of the Holy Spirit. Please let this gift be for Your glory and the benefit of people just like You did for the disciples who spoke the word of God with boldness in Acts, chapter 4. In Jesus' name, I pray, amen.

Activate:

Pair up with someone. Both of you take a moment to pray in the spirit. One person should volunteer to go first. As you pray in the spirit, ask God what He wants to do for the other person. The first person will place his or her hands on the second person and declare whatever God wants to impart at the moment. It could be peace, wisdom, courage, strength, joy, power, etc. Once you feel God has revealed His will, the person laying hands on the other person receiving should picture in their minds the presence of the Holy Spirit within themselves and a release of God's impartation to the other person. Now speak or declare verbally the impartation over your partner. After the first person finishes, then switch. (Note: if you are going to lay hands on anyone, please ask for permission. If the person receiving is not comfortable with the idea of laying hands on him or her, then pray without doing so). Laying hands on people is foundational to the Christian faith. It is a natural act that, when prompted by God, produces a supernatural result.[2]

2 Hebrews 6:1-2, 1Timothy 4:14, Acts 19:7; Mark 10:16; Acts 6:6, Acts 13:3

The Gifts of Healing

11

"to another gifts of healing by the one Spirit..."
1 Corinthians 12:9

Warm-up:

What are the benefits of a person being physically healthy? Share answers within the group as we discover the purpose of this gift.

Spotlight:

Through the gifts of healing, God grants us the ability to release the power to cure trauma, emotional, mental, and physical distress by praying, proclaiming, or laying hands-on people.

Read:

Acts 10:38 ESV
"How God anointed Jesus of Nazareth with the Holy Spirit and with power. He went about doing good and healing all who were oppressed by the devil, for God was with him."

Acts 3:2; 6-8; 12 ; 16 ESV
"And a man lame from birth was being carried, whom they laid daily at the gate of the temple that is called the Beautiful Gate to ask alms of those entering the temple."

"But Peter said, I have no silver and gold, but what I do have I give to you. In the name of Jesus Christ of Nazareth, rise up and walk!, And he took him by the right hand and raised him up, and immediately his feet and ankles were made strong. And leaping up, he stood and began to walk, and entered the temple with them, walking and leaping and praising God."

"And when Peter saw it he addressed the people: "Men of Israel, why do you wonder at this, or why do you stare at us, as though by our own power or piety we have made him walk?"

"And his name—by faith in his name—has made this man strong whom you see and know, and the faith that is through Jesus has given the man this perfect health in the presence of you all."

Discover:

Here, in Acts 10, Peter recounts the life of Jesus to Cornelius and his family. He tells them that while Jesus was on earth, He did good and healed people. Earlier, Jesus had promised that Peter and the other disciples would receive power to do what He did. God fulfilled the promise when He poured out His Spirit and 120 Christ-followers were baptized in power on Pentecost. These individuals boldly proclaimed the gospel and witnessed the growth of the church to 3,000, who they water baptized.

In the backdrop of the outpouring, Peter and John were on their way to join others at 3 pm for the hour of prayer. As they walked, they saw a poor man who had been crippled since birth, begging for money. As they passed him, their hearts, through faith, were filled with the sense that God wanted to heal the man. They told him that, while they didn't have any money, they did have the name or power of Jesus Christ, and in that name, they said, "Arise and walk." Peter laid hands on the man by taking his hand, and asked him to do something he could not do before, which is to stand up. As the man began standing, the power to cure his ailment was released. Strength filled his legs and joy, like he'd never known, filled his heart. God healed not only his body, but the joy was evidence that He cured this man's emotions and mind by the release of His healing power. The healing restored this man socially and gave him a chance to see his financial needs met in a way that restored his dignity. Peter and John clarified how the healing happened. They told the people that the cure was not because of their character or moral goodness. It was also not based on their own power and work. The healing came from Jesus' goodness and character and His power and work alone. The work that Jesus did on the cross provides forgiveness of sins and the healing of sickness. The man is made whole as a result of the gifts of healing at work through a verbal declaration of Jesus' name and an act of laying hands on the man which supplies God's power. Peter shows his faith in Jesus' goodness, work, and power through his actions. This power is the same power that raised Jesus from the dead. Thousands came to faith in Christ because this man was healed of a 40-year disease.

Application

Reflect:

1. What do gifts of healing reveal about God?

2. In what ways could this gift be beneficial for you and those around you?

3. Would you like to share any personal stories related to this gift?

Pray:

Heavenly Father, through the power of the Holy Spirit, please activate the gifts of healing in my life (or make them stronger in my life). Please allow this gift to be for Your glory and the benefit of people just like You did for disciples who brought healing to the soul and body of the lame man in Acts 3. In Jesus' name, I pray, amen.

Activate:

Ask if there is anyone in the group who would like to receive prayer for healing. If there's a need in the group, then do the steps below. If no one in the group needs healing, ask if anyone knows of someone outside of the group who needs healing. If so, take a moment to pray for that person in the spirit, and then, speak biblical scriptures about healing over that person.

If there is a need within the group, do the following:

- Ask the person what is the healing need they have that you can address.
- Invite God in by praying in the spirit, becoming aware of his presence in you, and asking Him to heal the person.
- Speak Biblical healing scriptures over the person (see appendix). Tell the pain, illness, or sickness to leave and speak healing to the issue, all in the name of Jesus Christ.
- Pray for God's love, joy, and peace to fill the person's life.
- Afterward, if possible, ask them to move or somehow test the part of their body that was sick. This question will help to activate the person's faith.
- Ask them how they feel on a scale of 1-10 before and after you have prayed. Don't be afraid to pray twice or three times. Sometimes it takes multiple times to see healing take place as it did for Jesus and the blind man.[1]
- If there is opposition, take a moment to pray through it. Ask God to help you to see if there is a hindrance, such as a sin or unforgiveness.[2]
- If, after praying for healing, there is no noticeable difference, encourage them to continue to pursue encouragement from God through the scriptures (see appendix). If there is a noticeable difference, then give God praise because it is His power and name that has

1 Mark 8:22-26
2 James 5:13-16

made this person well.

- End with a time of thanksgiving and prayer.

The Gift of Miracles

12

"to another the working of miracles..."
1 Corinthians 12:10 ESV

Warm-up:

Have you ever heard of a miracle from a family member or friend, or witnessed one in your life? Share answers within the group as we discover the purpose of this gift.

Spotlight:

Through the gift of miracles, God grants us the ability to bring about an instantaneous manifestation that accelerates or defies the ordinary course of nature. This manifestation comes through prayer, words, and actions inspired by the Holy Spirit and it results in confirmation of the gospel message.

Read:

Mark 5:35-42 NIV

"While Jesus was still speaking, some people came from the house of Jairus, the synagogue leader. 'Your daughter is dead,' they said. 'Why bother the teacher anymore?' Overhearing what they said, Jesus told him, 'Don't be afraid; just believe.' He did not let anyone follow him except Peter,

James, and John, the brother of James. When they came to the home of the synagogue leader, Jesus saw a commotion, with people crying and wailing loudly. He went in and said to them, 'Why all this commotion and wailing? The child is not dead but asleep.' But they laughed at him. After he put them all out, he took the child's father and mother and the disciples who were with him and went in where the child was. He took her by the hand and said to her, 'Talitha koum!' (which means 'Little girl, I say to you, get up!'). Immediately the girl stood up and began to walk around (she was twelve years old). At this, they were completely astonished."

Acts 9:39-40 NIV
"Peter went with them, and when he arrived, he was taken upstairs to the room. All the widows stood around him, crying and showing him the robes and other clothing that Dorcas had made while she was still with them. Peter sent them all out of the room; then he got down on his knees and prayed. Turning toward the dead woman, he said, 'Tabitha, get up.' She opened her eyes, and seeing Peter she sat up."

Discover:

Jesus consistently used the gift of miracles in His earthly ministry to reveal God's glory so people could believe in Him. He worked miracles that overturned threatening weather conditions, financial lack, demonic influence, sickness and disease, and much more.[1] Perhaps some of Jesus' greatest miracles involved raising the dead. After delivering a man who was controlled by a demon and healing a lady who had internal bleeding for years, Jesus found Himself in the house of Jairus, the synagogue leader.[2] Jairus' daughter, who was sick, had just died. As

1 Luke 8:22-25; Matthew 17:27; Luke 8:26-39
2 Luke 8:22-56

Jairus began to grieve his daughter's death, Jesus, whose faith was energized by the Holy Spirit, declared to him in essence, "Don't be afraid, let your faith meet My will." Jesus then proclaimed to all those who were mourning that the child was asleep and He put them out of the house because of their doubt and unbelief. Jesus sensed God's will for the situation. He responded in confidence with instructions from the Holy Spirit to take her by the hand and tell her to get up. The miracle came about, and her spirit returned to her body, bringing her back to life again.

Years later, his disciple Peter would take a page from Jesus' book and do the same things with Dorcas (or Tabitha). In Acts, chapter 9, we find Peter kneeling before the Heavenly Father and praying and praying and praying just like Jesus did with Jarius' daughter. In prayer, Peter discovers God's will and is infused with faith to release the gift of miracles. Tabitha came back to life, just like Jairus' daughter. With Peter and Jesus, the gift of faith was likely at work along with the gift of miracles. We also find that the gift of healing was at work as well. In both situations, God restored a loved one to her family and friends. As a result of the miracle, many rejoiced in the Lord, and the region received the gospel of Jesus Christ. The gift of miracles is a sign and wonder that confirms the message of God's kingdom and His love that Jesus and His followers shared with the world.

Application

Reflect:

1. How does the gift of miracles display God's glory?

2. In what ways could this gift be beneficial for you and those around you?

3. Would you like to share any personal stories related to this gift?

Pray:

Heavenly Father, through the power of the Holy Spirit, please activate the gift of miracles in my life (or make it stronger in my life). Please allow this gift to be used for Your glory and the benefit of people just like You did throughout the whole Bible. In Jesus name, I pray, amen.

Activate:

Each person should share a situation requiring a miraculous intervention from God. It could be a sickness or related to finances, relationships, etc. and could be for you or someone you know. After everyone shares, the group should choose one situation to focus on. Then, as a group, please take five or more minutes to pray in the spirit. Look for God to prompt you with courage and faith while you pray. Look for the Holy Spirit to bring scriptures to you. Next, speak what you perceive is God's desire directly to the situation. If you receive scriptures, proclaim them as well. End the time by giving God praise and praying a blessing over all the needs of the group.

What’s Next?

Grow in the Spiritual Gifts

Now that you've completed this guide, you may be asking, "What's next?". Paul's encouragement to Christ-followers was, "Follow the way of love and eagerly desire gifts of the Spirit, especially prophecy."[1] This scripture means that as we are motivated by love and God's glory, we should desire these spiritual gifts. I believe we can also apply this Bible passage to growth in these gifts. That is, we should seek to grow in the manifestation gifts of the Holy Spirit in order to love others and glorify Jesus. Here's how we grow:

We study the gifts of the Holy Spirit in scripture more.

> *"Do your best to present yourself to God as one approved, a worker who does not need to be ashamed and who correctly handles the word of truth." 2 Timothy 2:15*

From the beginning to the end of the Bible, God interacts with His people in supernatural ways. God endows men with gifts. Of course, we see the gifts are prominent in the ministry of Jesus Christ and His followers in the New

1 1 Corinthians 14:1

Testament. Go back through this study and read all related scriptures.

We pray in tongues or pray in the spirit regularly.

> *"But you, dear friends, by building yourselves up in your most holy faith and praying in the Holy Spirit, keep yourselves in God's love as you wait for the mercy of our Lord Jesus Christ to bring you to eternal life." Jude 20-21*

Praying in the spirit, particularly in tongues, builds you up in your faith.[2] Faith comes by revelation knowledge, so when you pray in tongues, this is one way you position yourself to receive revelation from God. Revelation releases faith and faith is required to practice the gifts of the Holy Spirit.

We make disciples of Jesus Christ by helping others to take their next steps with God.

> *"Therefore go and make disciples of all nations, baptizing them in the name of the Father and of the Son and of the Holy Spirit, and teaching them to obey everything I have commanded you. And surely I am with you always, to the very end of the age." Matthew 28:19-20*

The gifts of the Holy Spirit show up in our lives, and God strengthens them in us as we make disciples of Jesus Christ. Jesus said that He would be with us through the Holy Spirit when we make disciples. He also said we would receive the Holy Spirit's power to be a witness so we can win the world.

We bless our local church by serving and practicing

---

2 1 Corinthians 14:4

our gifts in the church according to the guidelines of our spiritual leaders.

> *"Each of you should use whatever gift you have received to serve others, as faithful stewards of God's grace in its various forms. If anyone speaks, they should do so as one who speaks the very words of God. If anyone serves, they should do so with the strength God provides, so that in all things God may be praised through Jesus Christ. To him be the glory and the power for ever and ever. Amen."*
> *1 Peter 4:10-11*

God intended for these gifts to be used in the context of blessing Christ-followers and reaching those who do not know Christ. We must practice these gifts in a way that blesses our church family, fits with our pastor's guidelines, and achieves our church's mission.

Lastly, always remember that these spiritual gifts do not define us or identify us.

These gifts are simply God's equipment to help us achieve His mission. We define ourselves as sons and daughters of the Heavenly Father and followers, friends, and servants of Jesus Christ. We should be thankful for the gifts, but we should rejoice more in the fact that we have eternal life because we belong to the Heavenly Father, Jesus, and Holy Spirit. Never forget what Jesus Christ said to His followers after they displayed His power in ministry:

> *"The seventy-two returned with joy and said, 'Lord, even the demons submit to us in your name.' He replied, 'I saw Satan fall like lightning from heaven. I have given you authority*

to trample on snakes and scorpions and to overcome all the power of the enemy; nothing will harm you. However, do not rejoice that the spirits submit to you, but rejoice that your names are written in heaven.'" Luke 10:17-20

Appendix

Salvation Prayer

Heavenly Father, thank you for creating and loving me. I confess I am a sinner and I ask you to forgive me. Jesus, I believe you died for my sins and rose from the dead. I receive you as my Lord and Savior; thank you for making me a new person. Holy Spirit, take my life and help me to follow you and to do Your will. In Jesus' name, amen.

Further Bible passages on the baptism of the Holy Spirit and manifestation gifts

Baptism of the Holy Spirit
Luke 3:21-22 & 4:16-21, John 7:37-39, Acts 1:1-8 & 2:1-4, Luke 24:36-48, Acts 8:14-25, Acts 9:10-17, Acts 10:34-48, Acts 19:1-11

Different kinds of tongues
Mark 16:17, 1 Corinthians 13:1, Acts 2:1-4, Acts 10:34-48, Acts 19:1-11, 1 Corinthians 14:1-40

Prophecy
Matthew 26:11-13, Matthew 21, 22, Luke 22:27-28, John 2:19, Acts 11:27-29, Acts 21:7-14

Interpretation of tongues
1 Corinthians 14:13-14, 27-28

Word of Wisdom
Matthew 22:15-22, Luke 4:1-14, Acts 15:1-21, Acts 6:1-7, Acts 23:6

Word of Knowledge
John 4:17-19* & 13-40, Acts 5:1-10, Acts 9:1-18

Distinguishing of spirits
Luke 13:10-13, Acts 8:22-23, Acts 16:1-18

Gift of Faith
Matthew 14:28-33, Mark 11:12-14 & 24, Matthew 21:21-22, James 1:5-8, 1 Corinthians 13:2

Gifts of Healings
Matthew 8:16,17, 1 Peter 2:24, Acts 9:32-35, Acts 28:7-10
Healing scriptures: Psalm 103:2-3, Isaiah 53:3-5, Proverbs 4:20-22

Gift of Miracles
John 2:1-11, Luke 8:43-48, Matthew 14:13-21, Acts 9:36-43, Acts 8:4-8

Different Categories of Spiritual Gifts

Name	Ministry Gifts	Manifestation Gifts	Motivational Gifts
Scripture	Ephesians 4:1-13; *11-12 (1 Corinthians 12:28-30)	1 Corinthians 12: 7-11	Romans 12:4-8
Key Word in Greek	Klesis (Calling)	Phanerosis (Manifestation)	Praxis (Action)
Nature	Vocational	Situational	Practical
Use	Purpose	Power	Practice
Purpose	Function	Equipment	Disposition
Alternate Name	a.ka. Fivefold plus other ministry gifts	a.k.a Miraculous	a.k.a Redemptive
Displays	God's government	God's eternal power	God's service
Motivation	Love	Love	Love

For more info about
Reggie Roberson checkout
www.heartreachglobal.org

Made in the USA
Columbia, SC
29 January 2024

31065475R00060